Forward

This collection of work is the culmination of a residency in 1992 [1-55]. Panayiotis Kalorkoti was commissioned by Cleveland County Council to portray and interpret the services provided for the people of Cleveland, by the County.

The initial idea for the residency developed from discussions between several groups within the Council: Libraries & Leisure Services, Cleveland Gallery, the Public Relations Department and from Cleveland Arts. There was strong support for a project which would go beyond simply documenting what takes place within the County, calling on the skill of the artist to observe and interpret.

Kalorkoti's experience of residencies, and his particular style of working, made him well-equipped to undertake such a project. In earlier writing about the artist's work, critics have made reference to the element of construction within his work, of Kalorkoti's ability to combine information and commentary with effect.

The logistics of the initial work are impressive: Kalorkoti travelled extensively throughout the County. He attended a wide range of activities and situations in more than forty sections and departments of the council. The resultant work developed into the rich body of drawings and etchings.

The residency aims to make an important point, that services are about people - Kalorkoti's 'images of Cleveland' are concerned with the individuals involved in all aspects of the County's work - in Education, Social Services, Libraries and Leisure and in the Fire and Police Services.

The drawings display a deceptive simplicity of structure. One of the strengths of Kalorkoti's work is that the image often goes no further than to portray the individual. Further information about environment and activity might be given by the figure's dress or uniform. In many drawings, we are confronted only by the face of the individual and yet, the personality has been captured. In four drawings [41-44], the artist introduces us to faces which seem familiar.

Kalorkoti has organised the information which he wishes to convey and is sufficiently confident in his technique to do so through the most straightforward of means. He is an accomplished communicator, using visual language in a way which means information is often implied rather than stated.

We can explore this approach in the eight etching's, where Kalorkoti's method of placing one image against the next, creates a multi-framed composition. In a work entitled 'People', the individual is juxtaposed against a map of Cleveland, thus placing the figure within the geographical location of the County. A second work, 'Landscape', brings several people engaged in various activities to the foreground of the work. A series of 'grid-lines' connect the individuals with the buildings which form the horizon of the image.

Kalorkoti's work is rich in information, but he decides how much to offer, so that as viewers we are not the passive recipients of this information, rather, we become involved in the process of interpretation.

Since the completion of the Cleveland residency, Kalorkoti has been concerned with the development of ideas and images from earlier work. The recent work, made in the artist's studio, forms the second part of the publication [56 - 92].

Jane Warrilow
Exhibitions Officer, Cleveland Gallery.

PANAYIOTIS KALORKOTI

Etchings and Drawings

Cleveland Gallery, Middlesbrough

26 September - 31 October 1992

Steendrukkerij Amsterdam B.V.

16 October - 21 November 1992

Westline Industrial Estates is an award winner under the Business Sponsorship Incentive Scheme for its support of Cleveland County Council. The BSIS is a Government Scheme administered by the Association for Business Sponsorship of the Arts.

KALORKOTI: the same side of the coin

His colours are not what you would describe as English, fortunately. This advantage can be put down to his Cypriot origin. His colours are intense, not primary but intense.

This quality of intensity applies to his work as a whole. Each etching has a direct and powerful effect, and gives the impression that it is about to reveal meanings and intentions. But on continued inspection we realize that what holds our gaze is pure illusion. Still, many of the images raise a smile of amusement: I experience pleasure in every etching he makes.

Every artist is, of course, an expressionist in a certain sense. The artist makes his work, in all seriousness, when the need is there. Whether or not pleasure is involved generally remains undiscussed. But Kalorkoti makes etchings in which pleasure is not just something incidental: rather, it is present like a basement under the whole picture surface.

Events materialize beyond the bounds of the image. The figure of a woman clad in underwear descends a staircase, her head invisible beyond the edge of the picture. Portraits seem at first to look us in the eye, whereas in reality their gaze is directed above or alongside us.

They are images which make us into observers of matters which catch our interest in a way which is purportedly unintended and unnoticed. In the mean-time, we are taken into their confidence. The granted intimacy makes us into a chosen elite and as a result our interest becomes even more acute. Yet in the end we are told nothing. We see a dispassionate tension, total in its seriousness and smouldering with irony.

The work of 1991 and 1992 condenses that of previous years. The works give the impression of being larger. The imagery is more monumental. There is a greater sensibility and thus also greater intensity.

Even more than was the case until recently, his blend of actions, vision and underlying assumptions generates work which displays a considerable exactness of image and technique while at the same time giving an impression of having arisen casually in an unconcentrated moment. The image behaves itself in a self-evident way, apparently effortless in its complexity.

Although Kalorkoti has produced delightful draw-ings, he does not accord them the same importance as his printed graphics. His drawings are all portraits and were made on location, outside the studio. The

KALORKOTI: dezelfde kant van de medaille

Zijn kleurgebruik kun je niet zuiver Engels noemen, gelukkig; dat is het voordeel dat hij van Cyprus afkomstig is.Zijn kleuren zijn helder, afgemengd maar helder.

Helder is het werk in zijn geheel te noemen. Elke ets heeft een directe en sterke werking en geeft de indruk betekenissen en bedoelingen prijs te geven, maar blijven kijken leert ons dat het enkel illusies zijn die ons in hun greep houden. Toch wekken veel beelden de lach op: ik geniet bij elke ets van zijn hand.

Iedere kunstenaar is in zekere zin natuurlijk expres-sionist. In alle ernst produceert hij als er een noodzaak is, maar of er misschien ook genot mee gemoeid is, komt meestal niet ter sprake. Kalorkoti levert etsen waar het genot niet zonder noodzaak is, en als een kelder onder het gehele oppervlak van het beeld aanwezig is.

Handelingen grijpen plaats buiten het beeld: een vrouwen-gestalte in ondergoed een trap afdalend, waarbij haar hoofd buiten de beelduitsnijding blijft; portretten die ons een blik lijken toe te werpen, maar in werkelijkheid vlak over ons heen of vlak naast ons kijken.

Het zijn beelden die ons tot toeschouwer maken van zaken die zogenaamd onbedoeld en ongemerkt onze belangstelling wekken. Ondertussen zijn wij in vertrouwen genomen. Het geschonken vertrouwen maakt ons tot uitverkorenen waardoor onze belangstelling nog intenser wordt. Vervolgens wordt ons niets meegedeeld. We zien een doodkalme span-ning, vol van ernst, smeulend van ironie.

In 1991 en 1992 zijn de werken uit de voorgaande jaren gecondenseerd; de werken zijn groter van aanpak, monumentaler in hun beeld; de sensibiliteit is toegenomen en daarmee de intensiteit.

Meer nog dan tot voor kort het geval was, zijn handeling, visie en uitgangspositie in hun samensmelting leverancier van werken die een grote exactheid in beeld en werkwijze tonen, terwijl ze tegelijkertijd de indruk wekken in momenten van achteloosheid te ontstaan. Het beeld voegt zich op een vanzelfsprekende manier, schijnbaar moeiteloos in zijn complexiteit.

Hoewel er prachtige tekeningen van zijn hand zijn, kent hij er niet het gewicht aan toe van zijn grafische werk. Alle tekeningen zijn portretten en ontstaan op lokatie, buiten het atelier. De tekeningen zijn registraties van wat, respectievelijk wie, zich aandient

drawings are registrations of whatever, or whoever, he encounters outside the studio, during journeys or in periods when he is not working on his etchings. The drawings show something of the same calm and remorselessness as those of Holbein or Ingres. By studying his oeuvre we can recognize the importance of the drawing work in his etchings.

Melted and congealed copies of figures and portraits, imagined ethnographic signs reminiscent of masks and fantasized graffiti, are torn from their recognizable context and float in image spaces and planes.

This is the inducement of pleasure.
It is the seriousness which instructs us to look again.
It is the mind floating above itself, parodying itself.

Frank Van den Broeck

Amsterdam,
1 August 1992

buiten het atelier, op reis of in periodes dat er geen etsen in behandeling zijn. De tekeningen tonen iets van de rust en de meedogenloosheid van de tekeningen van Holbein of Ingres. Wie zich in zijn oeuvre verdiept ziet het belang van de tekening in de etsen terug.

Gesmolten en gestolde kopieën van gestalten en portretten, verzonnen etnografica voor maskers, gefantaseerde schuttingtekeningen, losgetrokken uit hun vertrouwde context, zwevend in beeldende ruimten en vlakken.

Dit is het uitlokken van het genot.
Het is de ernst die ons wijst: kijk nogmaals.
Het is de geest boven zichzelf, zichzelf parodiërend.

Frank Van den Broeck

Amsterdam
1 augustus 1992

Drawings
and
Etchings

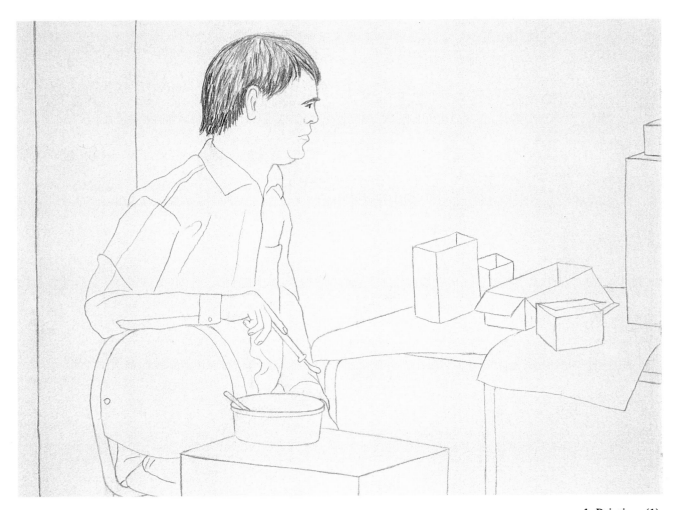

1. Painting (1)

2. Painting (2)

3. Work (1)

4. Work (2)

5. Work (3)

6. The Listener

7. Child (1)

8. Child (2)

9. Child (3)

10. Child (4)

11. Child (5)

12. Child (6)

13. Child (7)

14. Policeman (1)

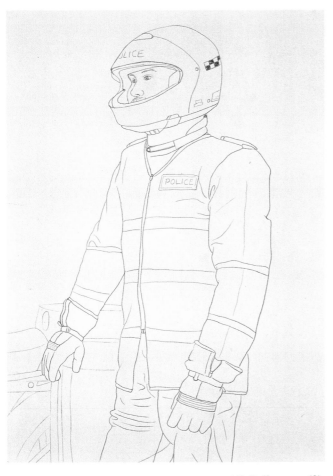

15. Policeman (2)

16. Policewoman

17. Child (8)

18. Listen

19. Old Man (1)

20. Old Man (2)

21. Old Man (3)

22. Old Man (4)

23. Old Man (5)

24. Old Man (6)

25. Old Man (7)

26. Worker

27. Fireman (1)

28. Fireman (2)

29. Fireman (3)

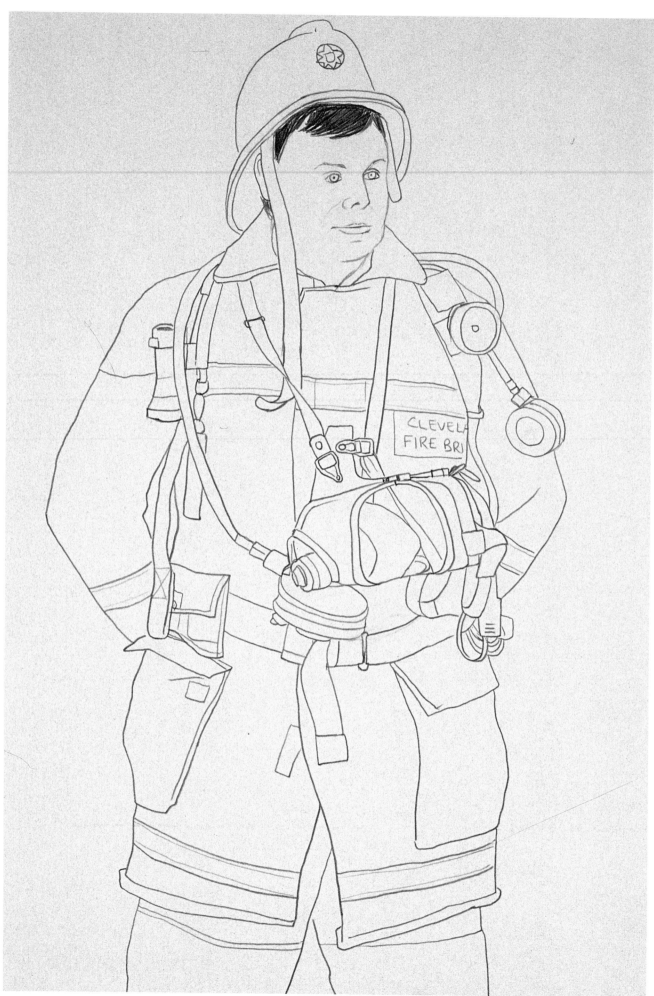

30. Fireman (4)

31. Fireman (5)

32. Fireman (6)

33. Fireman (7)

34. Fireman (8)

35. Drawing seq. no. 35

36. Drawing seq. no. 84

37. Study seq. no. 36

38. Study seq. no. 44

39. Study seq. no. 57

40. Study seq. no. 72

41. Portrait seq. no. 7

42. Portrait seq. no. 80

43. Portrait seq. no. 108

44. Portrait seq. no. 147

45. Still

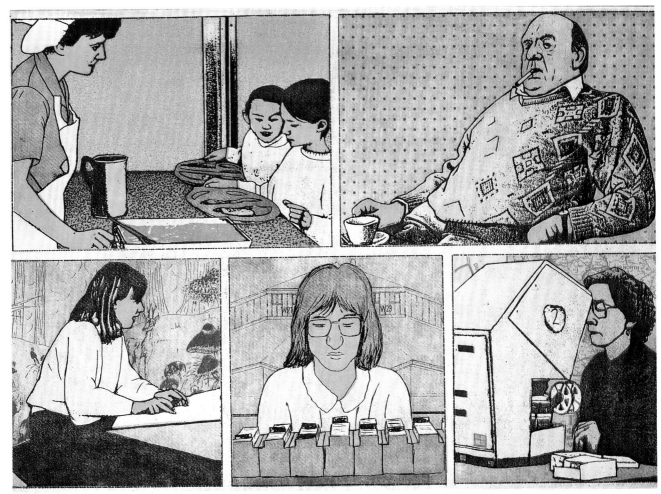

46. Knowledge

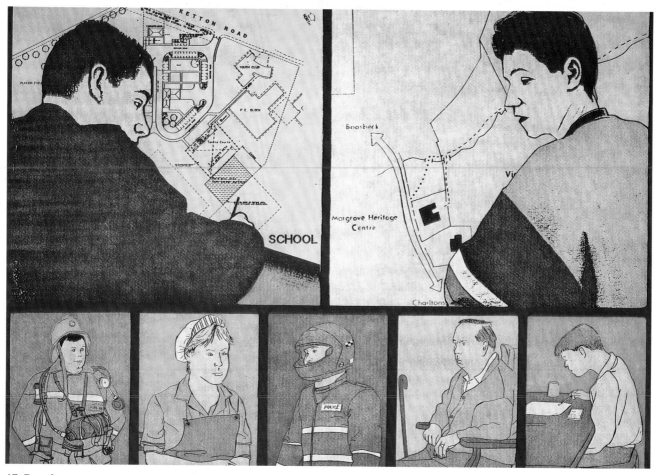

47. People

48. Landscape

50. Scenes

51. Reflections on a Composition

52. Detail: Reflections on a Composition

53. School

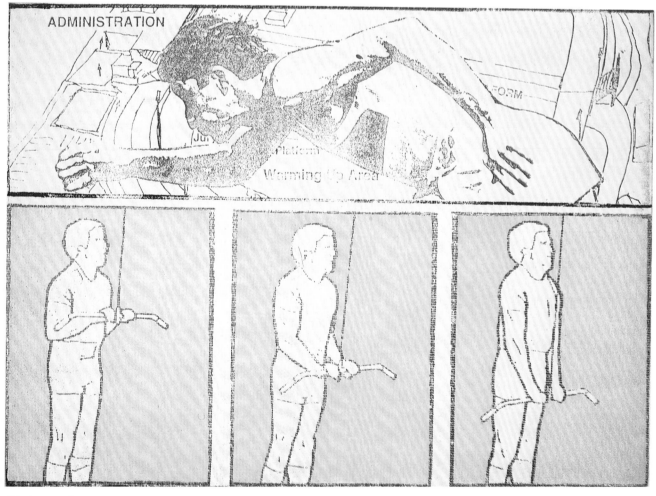

54. Attempting

56. Masks 1

57. Masks 2

58. Masks 3

59. Masks 4

60. Masks 5

61. Masks 6

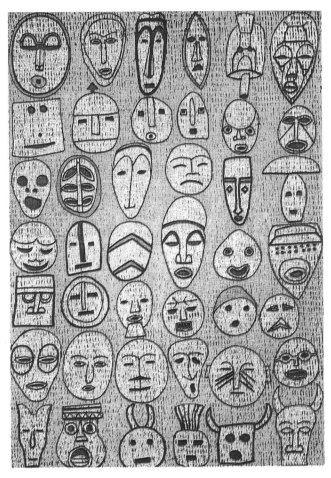

62. Masks 7

63. Masks 8

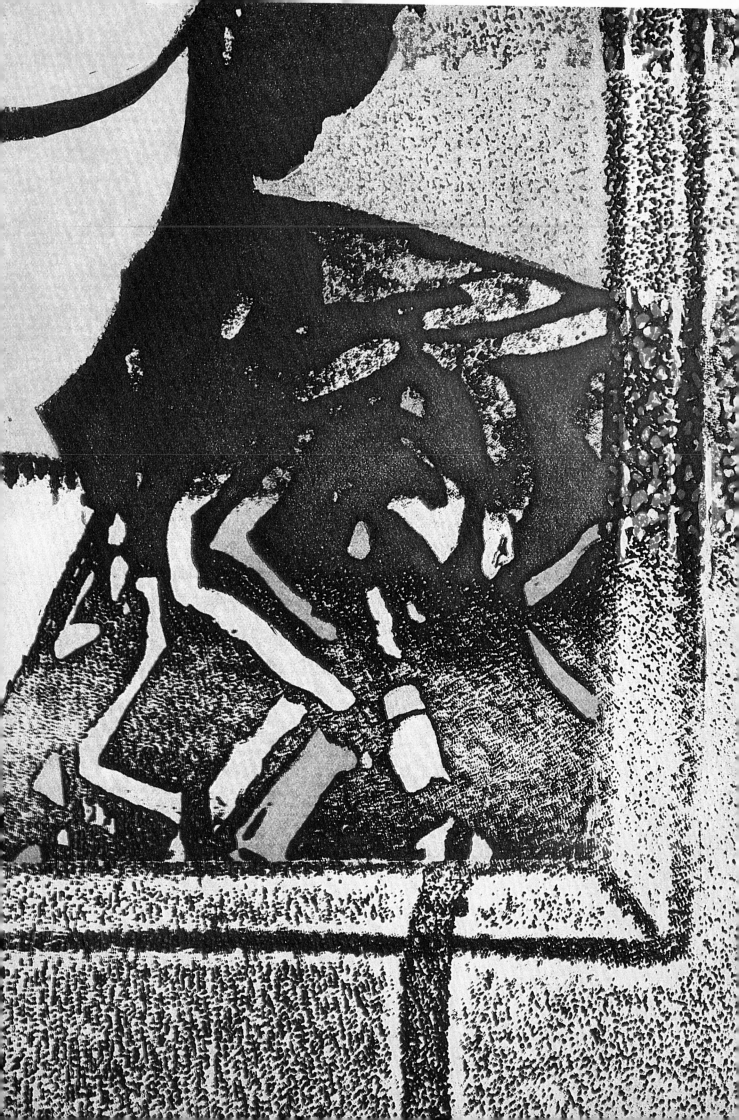

65. Untitled Portrait 1

64. Detail: Untitled Portrait 1

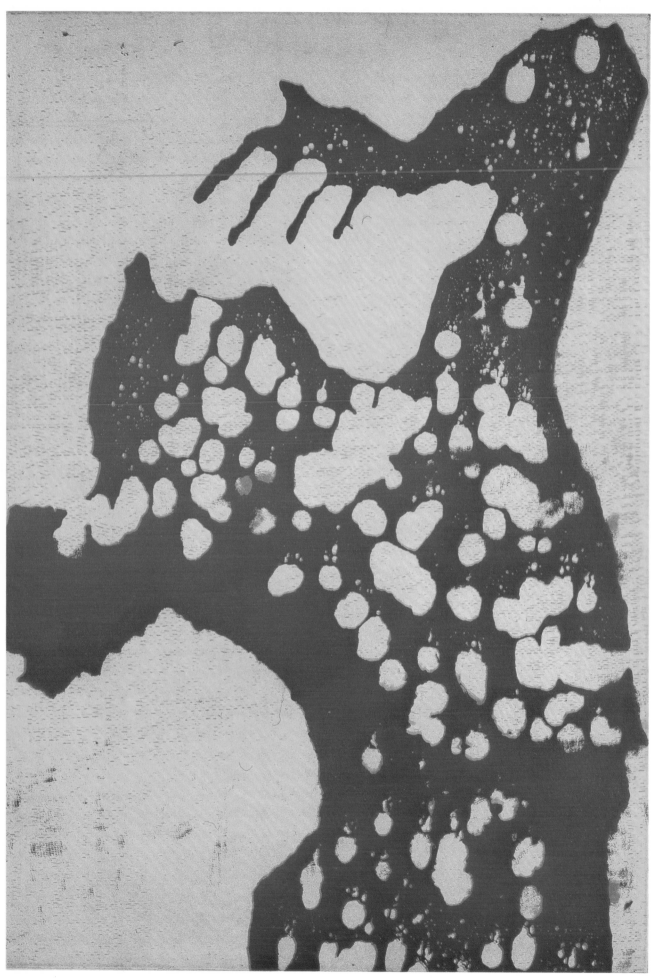

66. Untitled Portrait 2

67. Untitled Portrait 3

68. Untitled Portrait 4

69. Untitled Portrait 5

70. Untitled Portrait 6

71. Untitled Portrait 7

72. Untitled Portrait 8

73. Head 1

74. Head 2

75. Head 3

76. Head 4

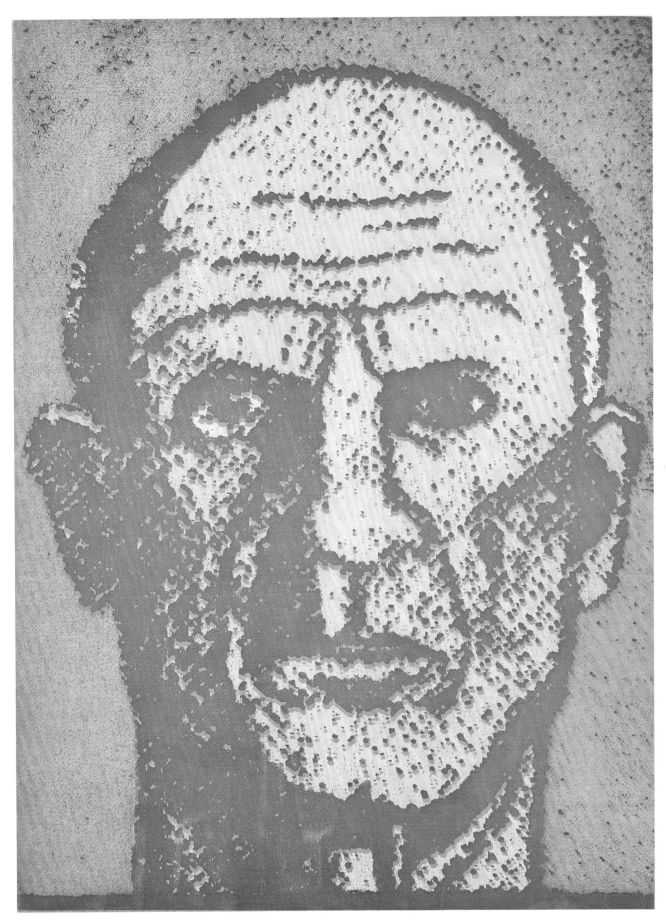

77. Head 5

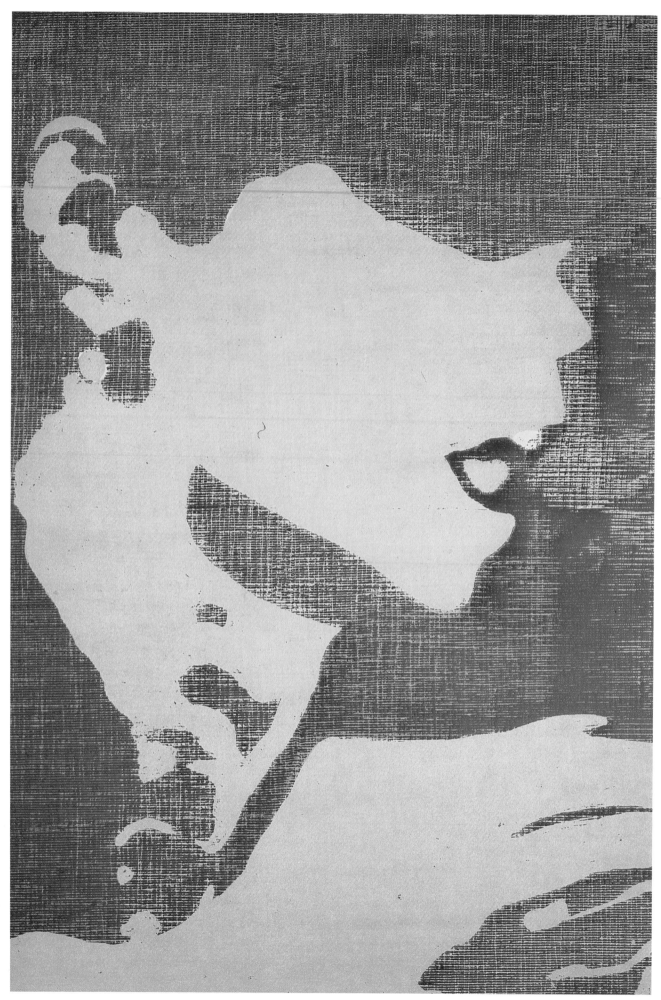

78. Head 6

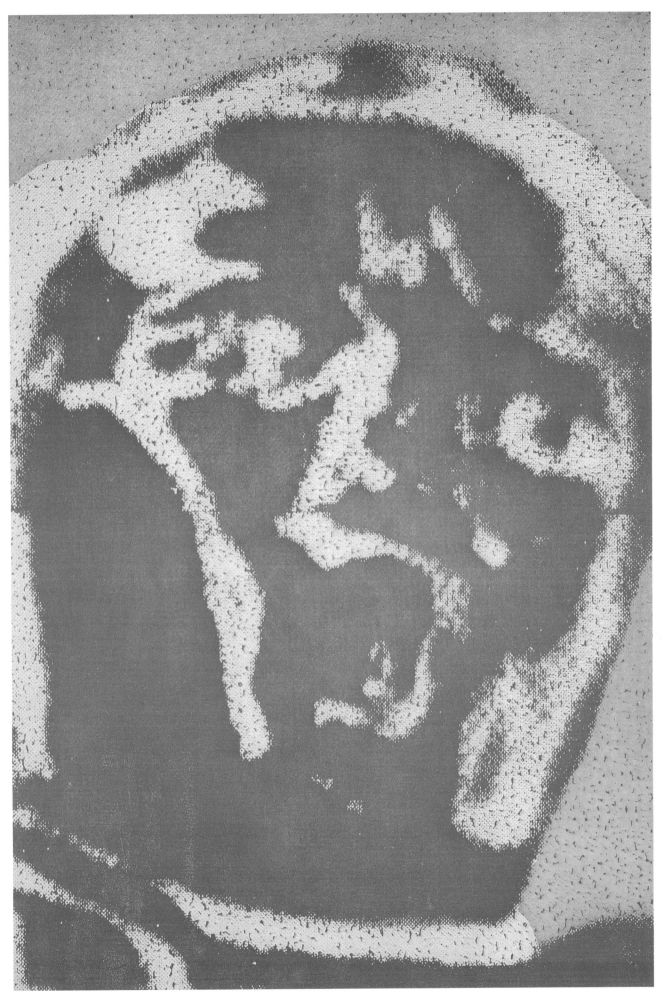

79. Head 7

80. Head 8

81. Detail: Head 8

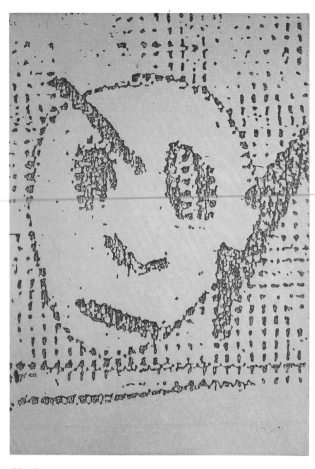

82. Study 1

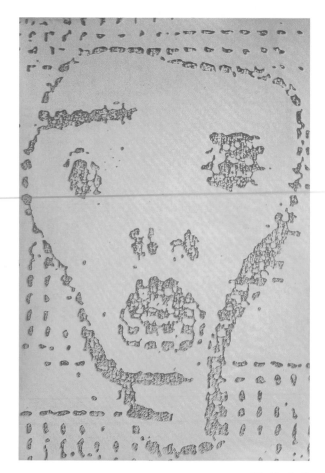

83. Study 2

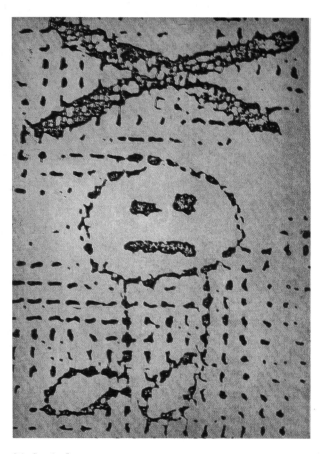

84. Study 3

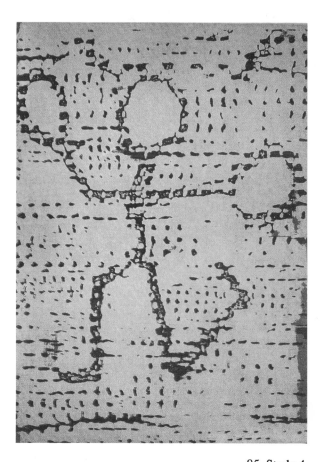

85. Study 4

86. Detail: Study 2

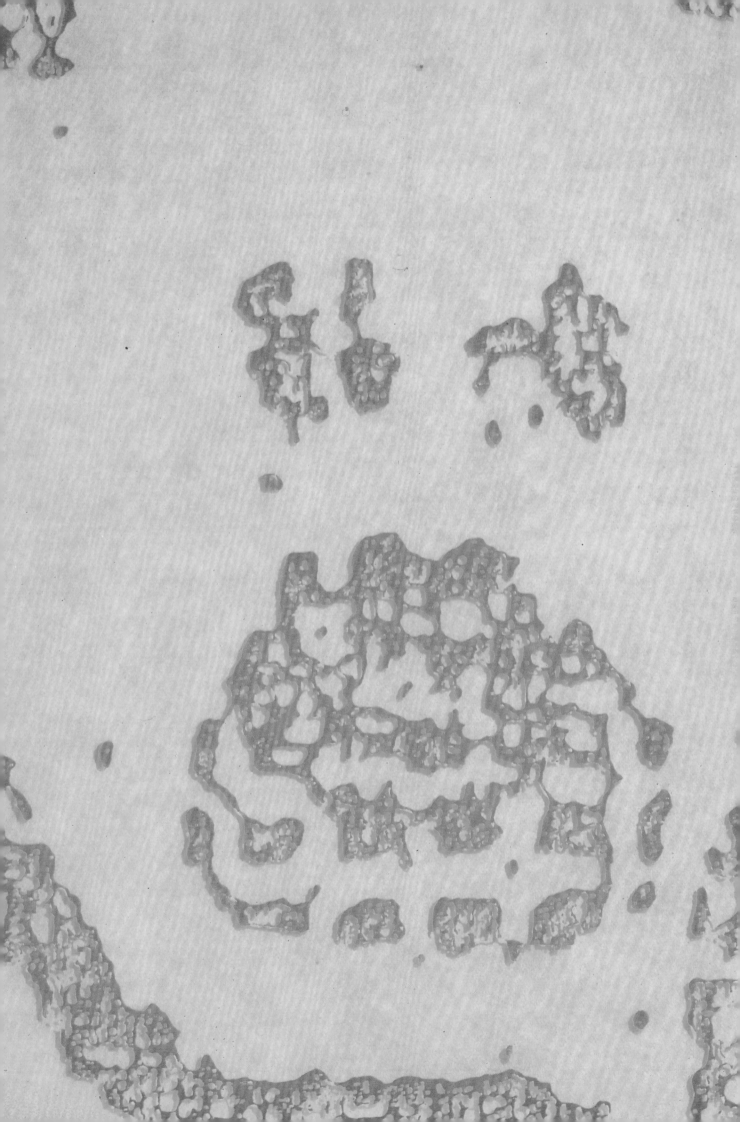

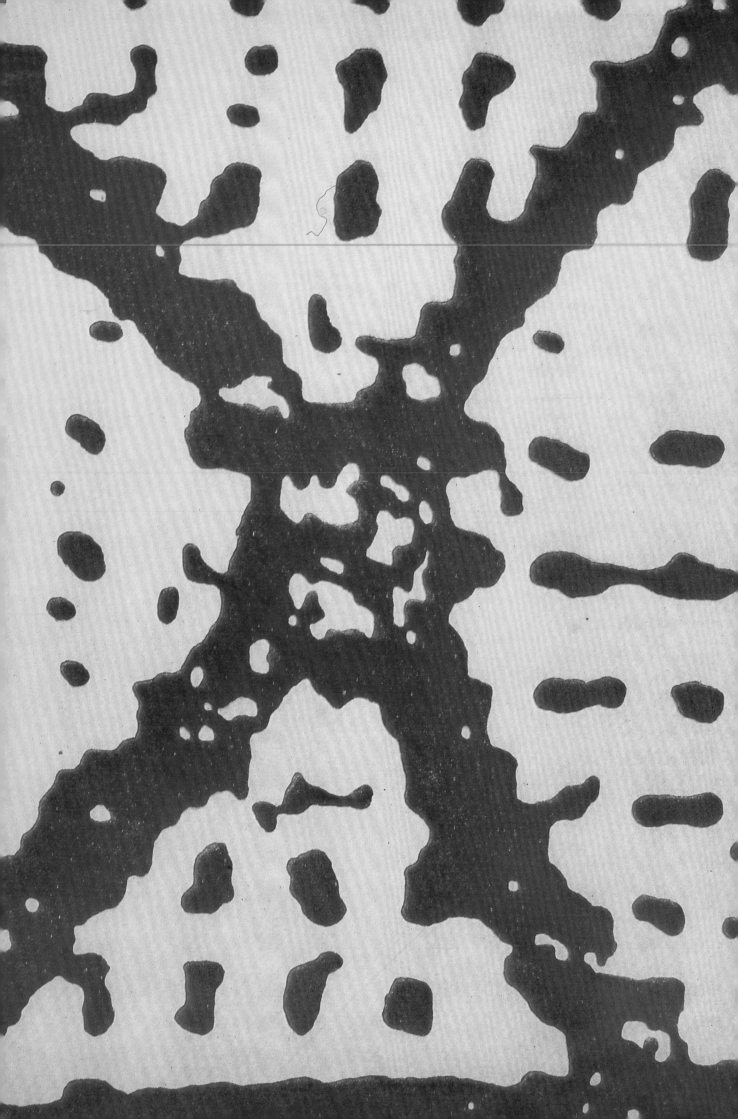

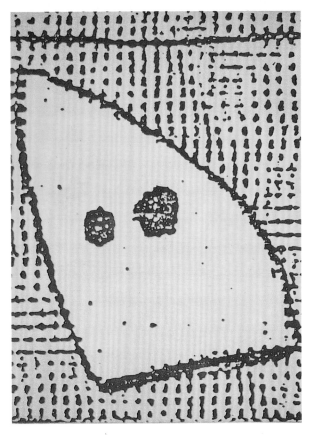

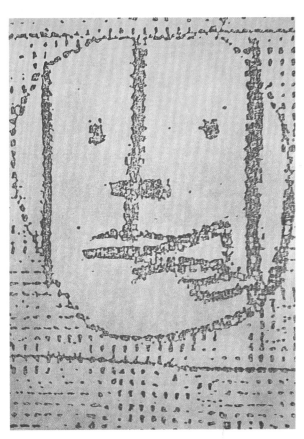

88. Study 5

89. Study 6

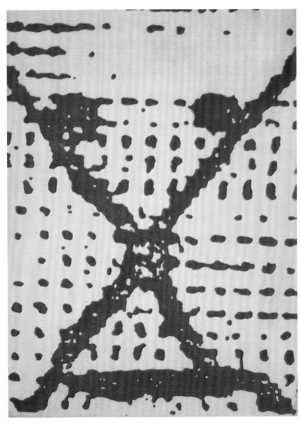

90. Study 7

91. Study 8

87. Detail: Study 7

92. Detail: Masks 4

List of Works

CLEVELAND RESIDENCY

1
Painting (1) 1992
(Allensway Centre)
Pencil on Paper
27.7 x 38.5cm (10^7/$_8$ x 15^1/$_8$ in)

2
Painting (2) 1992
(Allensway Centre)
Pencil on Paper
27.4 x 38.5cm (10^3/$_4$ x 15^1/$_8$ in)

3
Work (1) 1992
(Allensway Centre)
Pencil on Paper
29.7 x 41.3cm (11^{11}/$_{16}$ x 16^1/$_4$ in)

4
Work (2) 1992
(Allensway Centre)
Pencil on Paper
27.7 x 38.5cm (10^7/$_8$ x 15^1/$_8$ in)

5
Work (3) 1992
(Force Control)
Pencil on Paper
29.7 x 41.3cm (11^{11}/$_{16}$ x 16^1/$_4$ in)

6
The Listener 1992
(County Surgery)
Pencil on Paper
29.7 x 41.3cm (11^{11}/$_{16}$ x 16^1/$_4$ in)

7
Child (1) 1992
(Easterside School)
Pencil on Paper
41.3 x 29.7cm (16^1/$_4$ x 11^{11}/$_{16}$ in)

8
Child (2) 1992
(Easterside School)
Pencil on Paper
41.3 x 29.7cm (16^1/$_4$ x 11^{11}/$_{16}$ in)

9
Child (3) 1992
(De Brus School)
Pencil on Paper
37.8 x 26.4cm (14^7/$_8$ x 10^7/$_8$ in)

10
Child (4) 1992
(De Brus School)
Pencil on Paper
37.5 x 26.7cm (14^3/$_4$ x 10^1/$_2$ in)

11
Child (5) 1992
(Easterside School)
Pencil on Paper
29.7 x 41.3cm (11^{11}/$_{16}$ x 16^1/$_4$ in)

12
Child (6) 1992
(Easterside School)
Pencil on Paper
29.7 x 41.3cm (11^{11}/$_{16}$ x 16^1/$_4$ in)

13
Child (7) 1992
(Hemlington Library)
Pencil on Paper
29.7cm x 41.3cm (11^{11}/$_{16}$ x 16^1/$_4$ in)

14
Policeman (1) 1992
Pencil on Paper
26.7 x 37.5cm (10^1/$_2$ x 14^3/$_4$ in)

15
Policeman (2) 1992
Pencil on Paper
38.1 x 28.3cm (15 x 11^1/$_8$ in)

16
Policewoman 1992
Pencil on Paper
41.3 x 29.7cm (16^1/$_4$ x 11^{11}/$_{16}$ in)

17
Child (8) 1992
(Easterside School)
Pencil on Paper
37.5 x 26.4cm (14^3/$_4$ x 10^3/$_8$ in)

18
Listen 1992
Pencil on Paper
41.3 x 29.7cm (16^1/$_4$ x 11^{11}/$_{16}$ in)

19
Old Man (1) 1992
(Day Centre)
Pencil on Paper
38.1 x 27.7cm (15 x 10^7/$_8$ in)

20
Old Man (2) 1992
(Day Centre)
Pencil on Paper
38.1 x 27.7 cm (15 x 10^7/$_8$ in)

21
Old Man (3) 1992
(Day Centre)
Pencil on Paper
38.1 x 27.4 cm (15 x 10^3/$_4$ in)

22
Old Man (4) 1992
(Day Centre)
Pencil on Paper
38.1 x 27.4 cm (15 x 10^3/$_4$ in)

23
Old Man (5) 1992
(Day Centre)
Pencil on Paper
37.9 x 26.4cm (14^7/$_8$ x 10^3/$_8$ in)

24
Old Man (6) 1992
(Day Centre)
Pencil on Paper
37.9 x 26.4cm (14^7/$_8$ x 10^3/$_8$ in)

25
Old Man (7) 1992
(Day Centre)
Pencil on Paper
37.9 x 26.4cm (14^7/$_8$ x 10^3/$_8$ in)

26
Worker 1992
Pencil on Paper
41.3 x 29.7cm (16^1/$_4$ x 11^{11}/$_{16}$ in

27
Fireman (1) 1992
Pencil on Paper
38.1 x 28.3 cm (15 x 11^1/$_8$ in)

28
Fireman (2) 1992
Pencil on Paper
38.1 x 28.3 cm (15 x 11^1/$_8$ in)

29
Fireman (3) 1992
Pencil on Paper
38.1 x 28.3 cm (15 x 11^1/$_8$ in)

30
Fireman (4) 1992
Pencil on Paper
38.1 x 28.3 cm (15 x 11^1/$_8$ in)

31
Fireman (5) 1992
Pencil on Paper
38.7 x 28.1 cm (15^1/$_4$ x 11^1/$_{16}$ in)

32
Fireman (6) 1992
Pencil on Paper
37.5 x 26.7cm (14^3/$_4$ x 10^1/$_2$ in)

33
Fireman (7) 1992
Pencil on Paper
41.3 x 29.7cm (16$^{1}/_{4}$ x 11$^{11}/_{16}$ in)

34
Fireman (8) 1992
Pencil on Paper
41.3 x 29.7cm (16$^{1}/_{4}$ x 11$^{11}/_{16}$ in)

35
Drawing:seq.no.35 1992
Pencil on Paper
9.3 x 14.4cm (3$^{7}/_{8}$ x 5$^{7}/_{8}$ in)

36
Drawing:seq.no.84 1992
Pencil on Paper
9.3 x 14.4cm (3$^{7}/_{8}$ x 5$^{7}/_{8}$ in)
37
Study:seq.no.36 1992
Pencil on Paper
14.1 x 19.7cm (5$^{9}/_{16}$ x 7$^{3}/_{4}$ in)

38
Study:seq.no.44 1992
Pencil on Paper
14.1 x 19.7cm (5$^{9}/_{16}$ x 7$^{3}/_{4}$ in)

39
Study:seq.no.57 1992
Pencil on Paper
14.1 x 19.7cm (5$^{9}/_{16}$ x 7$^{3}/_{4}$ in)

40
Study:seq.no.72 1992
Pencil on Paper
14.1 x 19.7cm (5$^{9}/_{16}$ x 7$^{3}/_{4}$ in)

41
Portrait:seq.no.7 1992
Pencil on Paper
14.1 x 10cm (5$^{9}/_{16}$ x 3$^{15}/_{16}$ in)

42
Portrait:seq.no.80 1992
Pencil on Paper
14.1 x 10cm (5$^{9}/_{16}$ x 3$^{15}/_{16}$ in)

43
Portrait:seq.no.108 1992
Pencil on Paper
14.1 x 10cm (5$^{9}/_{16}$ x 3$^{15}/_{16}$ in)

44
Portrait:seq.no.147 1992
Pencil on Paper
14.1 x 10cm (5$^{9}/_{16}$ x 3$^{15}/_{16}$ in)

45
Still 1992
Multi-Plate Etching
56.5 x 76.2cm (22$^{1}/_{4}$ x 30 in)
Edition of 10

46
Knowledge 1992
Multi-Plate Etching
56.5 x 76.2cm (22$^{1}/_{4}$ x 30 in)
Edition of 10

47
People 1992
Multi-Plate Etching
56.5 x 76.2cm (22$^{1}/_{4}$ x 30 in)
Edition of 10

48
Landscape 1992
Multi-Plate Etching
56.5 x 76.2cm (22$^{1}/_{4}$ x 30 in)
Edition of 10

49
Detail: **People**

50
Scenes 1992
Multi-Plate Etching
56.5 x 76.2cm (22$^{1}/_{4}$ x 30 in)
Edition of 10

51
Reflections on a Composition 1992
Multi-Plate Etching
56.5 x 76.2cm (22$^{1}/_{4}$ x 30 in)
Edition of 10

52
*Detail:***Reflections on a Composition**

53
School 1992
Multi-Plate Etching
56.5 x 76.2cm (22$^{1}/_{4}$ x 30 in)
Edition of 10

54
Attempting 1992
Multi-Plate Etching
56.5 x 76.2cm (22$^{1}/_{4}$ x 30 in)
Edition of 10

55
Detail: **School**

RECENT WORK

56
Masks 1 1990
Multi-Plate Etching
76.2 x 56.5 cm (30 x 22$^{1}/_{4}$ in)
Edition of 10

57
Masks 2 1990
Multi-Plate Etching
76.2 x 56.5 cm (30 x 22$^{1}/_{4}$ in)
Edition of 10

58
Masks 3 1990
Multi-Plate Etching
76.2 x 56.5 cm (30 x 22$^{1}/_{4}$ in)
Edition of 10

59
Masks 4 1990
Multi-Plate Etching
76.2 x 56.5 cm (30 x 22$^{1}/_{4}$ in)
Edition of 10

60
Masks 5 1990
Multi-Plate Etching
76.2 x 56.5 cm (30 x 22$^{1}/_{4}$ in)
Edition of 10

61
Masks 6 1990
Multi-Plate Etching
76.2 x 56.5 cm (30 x 22$^{1}/_{4}$ in)
Edition of 10

62
Masks 7 1990
Multi-Plate Etching
76.2 x 56.5 cm (30 x 22$^{1}/_{4}$ in)
Edition of 10

63
Masks 8 1990
Multi-Plate Etching
76.2 x 56.5 cm (30 x 22$^{1}/_{4}$ in)
Edition of 10

64
*Detail:***Untitled Portrait 1**

65
Untitled Portrait 1 1991
Multi-Plate Etching
76.2 x 56.5 cm (30 x 22$^{1}/_{4}$ in)
Edition of 10

66
Untitled Portrait 2 1991
Multi-Plate Etching
76.2 x 56.5 cm (30 x 22$^{1}/_{4}$ in)
Edition of 10

67
Untitled Portrait 3 1991
Multi-Plate Etching
76.2 x 56.5 cm (30 x 22$^{1}/_{4}$ in)
Edition of 10

68
Untitled Portrait 4 1991
Multi-Plate Etching
76.2 x 56.5 cm (30 x 22$^{1}/_{4}$ in)
Edition of 10

69
Untitled Portrait 5 1991
Multi-Plate Etching
76.2 x 56.5 cm (30 x 22¹/₄ in)
Edition of 10

70
Untitled Portrait 6 1991
Multi-Plate Etching
76.2 x 56.5 cm (30 x 22¹/₄ in)
Edition of 10

71
Untitled Portrait 7 1991
Multi-Plate Etching
76.2 x 56.5 cm (30 x 22¹/₄ in)
Edition of 10

72
Untitled Portrait 8 1991
Multi-Plate Etching
76.2 x 56.5 cm (30 x 22¹/₄ in)
Edition of 10

73
Head 1 1991
Multi-Plate Etching
76.2 x 56.5 cm (30 x 22¹/₄ in)
Edition of 10

74
Head 2 1991
Multi-Plate Etching
76.2 x 56.5 cm (30 x 22¹/₄ in)
Edition of 10

75
Head 3 1991
Multi-Plate Etching
76.2 x 56.5 cm (30 x 22¹/₄ in)
Edition of 10

76
Head 4 1991
Multi-Plate Etching
76.2 x 56.5 cm (30 x 22¹/₄ in)
Edition of 10

77
Head 5 1991
Multi-Plate Etching
76.2 x 56.5 cm (30 x 22¹/₄ in)
Edition of 10

78
Head 6 1991
Multi-Plate Etching
76.2 x 56.5 cm (30 x 22¹/₄ in)
Edition of 10

79
Head 7 1991
Multi-Plate Etching
76.2 x 56.5 cm (30 x 22¹/₄ in)
Edition of 10

80
Head 8 1991
Multi-Plate Etching
76.2 x 56.5 cm (30 x 22¹/₄ in)
Edition of 10

81
*Detail:***Head 8**

82
Study 1 1992
Multi-Plate Etching
76.2 x 56.5 cm (30 x 22¹/₄ in)
Edition of 10

83
Study 2 1992
Multi-Plate Etching
76.2 x 56.5 cm (30 x 22¹/₄ in)
Edition of 10

84
Study 3 1992
Multi-Plate Etching
76.2 x 56.5 cm (30 x 22¹/₄ in)
Edition of 10

85
Study 4 1992
Multi-Plate Etching
76.2 x 56.5 cm (30 x 22¹/₄ in)
Edition of 10

86
Detail: **Study 2**

87
Detail: **Study 7**

88
Study 5 1992
Multi-Plate Etching
76.2 x 56.5 cm (30 x 22¹/₄ in)
Edition of 10

89
Study 6 1992
Multi-Plate Etching
76.2 x 56.5 cm (30 x 22¹/₄ in)
Edition of 10

90
Study 7 1992
Multi-Plate Etching
76.2 x 56.5 cm (30 x 22¹/₄ in)
Edition of 10

91
Study 8 1992
Multi-Plate Etching
76.2 x 56.5 cm (30 x 22¹/₄ in)
Edition of 10

92
Detail: **Masks 4**

Detail: Fireman (4)

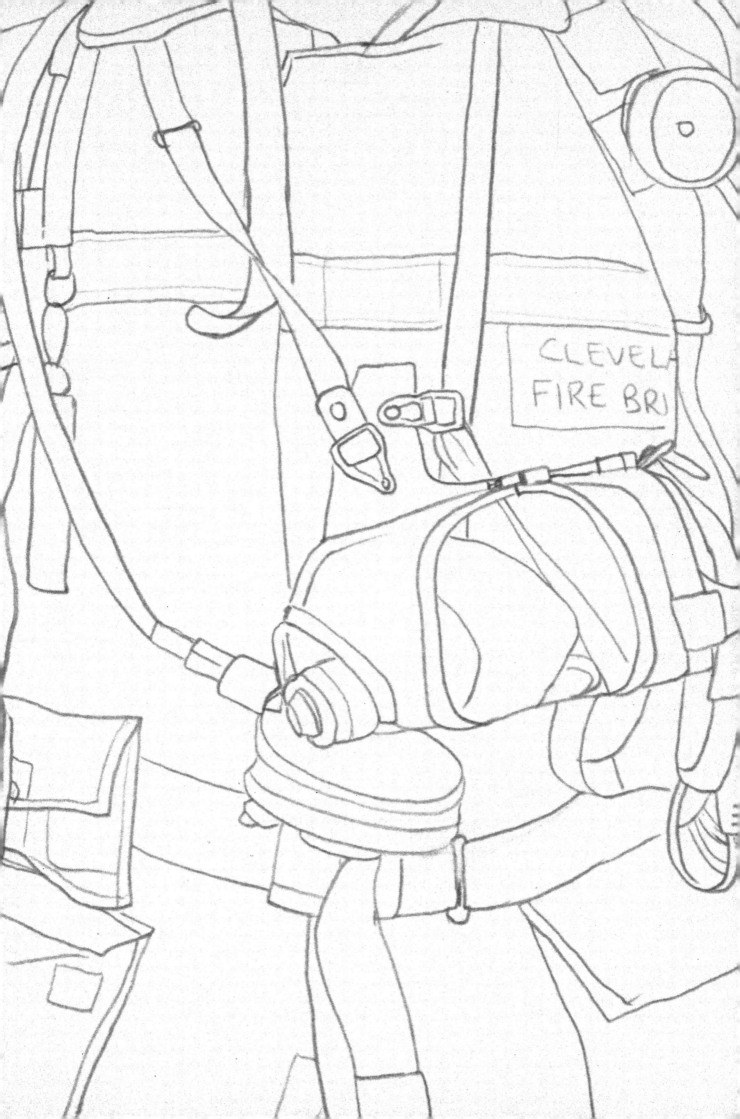

Biography

Born in Cyprus 1957

1976-80   Newcastle upon Tyne University, B.A. (Hons.)
1st Class in Fine Art

1982-85   Royal College of Art, London, M.A. in
Printmaking.

1985   Artist in Residence at Leeds Playhouse

1986-87   Koninklijke Akademie voor Kunst en
Vormgeving, 's-Hertogenbosch
(Netherlands Government Scholarship)

1988   Bartlett Fellow in the Visual Arts
(Newcastle upon Tyne University)

1991   Lowick House Bursary

1992   Artist in Residence, Cleveland County

Taught part-time and visiting Lecturer at a number of Art
Colleges

Commissions

1988   Imperial War Museum, London
People's Theatre, Newcastle

1989   Borough of Darlington
Borough of Hartlepool
Grizedale Society (Theatre in the Forest)

1990   National Garden Festival, Gateshead

1991   Grizedale Society (Theatre in the Forest)

Public Collections

Stedelijk Museum, Amsterdam
British Council
Imperial War Museum
Laing Art Gallery, Newcastle
Northern Arts
IBM
Rank Xerox

Solo Exhibitions

1980   Newcastle Polytechnic Gallery

1981   Bede Gallery, Jarrow
Hendersons Gallery, Edinburgh

1982   Bede Monastery Museum, Jarrow
Ceolfrith Gallery, Sunderland Arts Centre
Pentonville Gallery, London

1984   Abbot Hall Gallery, Kendal

1987   The Minories, Colchester
Steendrukkerij Amsterdam B.V.

1988-89 Hatton Gallery, Newcastle and tour: Darlington
Arts Centre; Gray Art Gallery and Museum,
Hartlepool; Queen's Hall Arts Centre, Hexham
(Catalogue)

1990   Imperial War Museum, London (Catalogue)
National Garden Festival, Gateshead (Catalogue)

1992   Design Works, Gateshead (Catalogue)
Cleveland Gallery, Middlesbrough and tour:
Steendrukkerij Amsterdam B.V. (Catalogue)

Group Exhibitions

1980   The Stone Gallery, Newcastle

1981   'Small Works' Newcastle Polytechnic Gallery

1982   'and Printmaking' Waterloo Gallery, London
(Catalogue)

1983   'Stowells Trophy' Royal Academy of Arts,
London
'Northern Young Contemporaries'
(awarded Granada Prize) Whitworth Art
Gallery, Manchester

1984   Bath Festival Painting Competition
'New Contemporaries' ICA, London (Catalogue)

1985   'Printmakers at the Royal College of Art'
Concourse Gallery, Barbican Centre, London
(Catalogue)
'Fresh Air' St. Paul's Gallery, Leeds
'Whitworth Young Contemporaries' Whitworth
Art Gallery, Manchester

1986   'Tradition and Innovation in Printmaking
Today' Concourse Gallery, Barbican Centre,
London and tour: Milton Keynes Exhibition
Gallery; Ferens Art Gallery, Hull; Andrew Grant
Gallery, Edinburgh; Aspex Gallery, Portsmouth
(Catalogue)
'Between Identity and Politics, A New Art'
Gimpel Fils, London and tour: Darlington Arts
Centre; Gimpel and Weitzenhoffer, New York
(Catalogue)
'Fresh Art' Concourse Gallery, Barbican
Centre, London (Catalogue)
'Whitechapel Open' Whitechapel Art Gallery,
London

1987   Athena Art Awards, Concourse Gallery,
Barbican Centre, London
'Which Side of the Fence' Imperial War
Museum, London

1989   'The Artistic Records Committee: A Retrospec-
tive 1972-1989' Imperial War Museum, London

1991   'Homage to Goya' and 'Soldier'
Museum of Modern Art, Oxford

Cover: People 1992
Copyright © Panayiotis Kalorkoti
ISBN 0 904784 21 5

Published in collaboration with Cleveland County Council
Photographs by Graham Oliver
Translation by V.J. Joseph, Amsterdam
Catalogue designed by Peter Morrill
Printed by Colden Offset Ltd.